CCSS **Genre** Realistic Fiction

Essential Question
How can we reuse what we already have?

The Great Book Swap

by Alan Mitchell • illustrated by Susan Lexa-Senning

"Mario, how is the cleanup going?" asks Mario's mom. "Our new house is smaller. You can't take everything."

"I can't **decide** which books to keep," says Mario.

"Keep your favorite books," says his mother.

Mario **gazes** at his bookcase. It is overflowing with too many books. He feels **discouraged**. He wants to keep all of his books.

Mario holds up a book about a vet. "This is not mine," he says.

"That was Selina's book. She wanted to be a vet after she read it," says his mother.

STOP AND CHECK

Why does Mario feel discouraged?

3

Then Mario's mother gives him a book. "This is yours," she says.

"*Amazing Robot Facts!* That's my favorite book," says Mario.

Mario's friend Sam comes over. Mario shows him the book.

"Remember when we **pretended** to be robots one weekend?" says Mario. "We wouldn't go to bed."

"That's because robots don't sleep," says Sam.

"Papa knew what to do," says Mario. "He said that robots have to obey orders that humans give them."

"My little brother would like this book. Are you giving it away?" asks Sam.

"No, it's my favorite," says Mario.

"Do you read books more than once?" asks Sam.

"Sometimes," says Mario. "I don't need to reread all of these, though. I could give them away."

STOP AND CHECK

Why is Mario sorting through his books?

Chapter 2
A Home Without Books

In class, Mario's teacher asks the students which books they like.

"I like *Amazing Robot Facts!*," says Mario.

"Rene, what's your favorite book?" asks the teacher.

"I don't like books. Books are old technology," says Rene. "I like the game *Wrestling Robots.*"

Mario wonders if books are really old technology.

"Mario, let's play *Wrestling Robots* at my house after school," says Rene after class.

"Okay," says Mario. "I'll bring the book about robots. We'll see which one is better."

At Rene's house, Mario plays *Wrestling Robots*. He looks around Rene's room. There are no books.

Later, Mario sees Rene's brother and sister. They are reading the robot book.

"I've learned lots of things about robots from this book," says Frankie **proudly**. He is **jubilant**.

"Everything?" asks Rene. "How do robots wrestle?"

Frankie doesn't want to stop reading the book. He sighs in **frustration** when he gives it back to Mario.

STOP AND CHECK

What is Rene's favorite book?

9

Chapter 3
Old Technology

The next day, Mario has a plan. He talks to his teacher.

"Miss Foster, can we have a book **swap**, please? Everyone can give away their old books and get other books in return. We could give the **remaining** books to the library."

"That's a great idea," says Miss Foster.

Mario and Sam make a flier about the book swap.

The Great
School Book Swap

Donate your old books and
take new books in return.

It will be Friday at 1:00 p.m.
in the school hall.

Leftover books will go to the library.

Miss Foster prints copies of the fliers.

Mario gives Rene a flier.

"No, thanks," says Rene. "I don't **bother** with old technology."

Mario remembers that there were no books at Rene's house. He talks to Miss Foster.

"Some people don't have any books to swap. Could they get a book if they help out?" asks Mario.

"Good idea," says Miss Foster.

Miss Foster asks if some students can help at the book swap.

Mario raises his hand. Rene does, too.

STOP AND CHECK

What is a book swap?

Chapter 4
Books for All

It is the day of the book swap. The school hall is full of books. A girl picks up *The Story of a Vet*.

"That was my sister's book," says Mario. "She is studying to be a vet."

"I can't wait to read it," says the girl.

Rene is in charge of a table of books. He calls Mario and Sam over. He has **tinkered** with his **display** and is proud of how it looks.

"You might like this one," says Rene. He holds up a book about cars.

"Thanks," says Mario. "I haven't read it."

Rene checks the book off a list. Mario sees a check next to *Amazing Robot Facts!*

Rene looks embarrassed.

"Did you choose that book for Frankie?" asks Mario.

"Yes," says Rene, smiling. "He doesn't know that books are old technology!"

STOP AND CHECK

Why is Rene embarrassed?

Respond to Reading

Summarize

Summarize *The Great Book Swap*. Use details from the story. Your chart may help you.

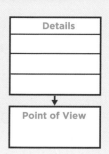

Details

↓

Point of View

Text Evidence

1. Reread page 7. Does Mario believe Rene when he says books are old technology? Use an example from the story in your answer. Point of View

2. What does the word *overflowing* on page 3 mean? What clues helped you? Vocabulary

3. Write about Mario and his feelings toward his books. How do these feelings change? Write About Reading

Compare Texts

Read about how to run a book swap.

Why Not Swap?

Do you like playing with your friends' toys? Do you like reading your friends' books? It's fun to have something different to play with. It's fun to read something different. Sometimes a new toy ends up in your closet. A new book sits in your bookcase.

Focus on Genre

Realistic Fiction Realistic fiction stories are often set in the present. The characters are like real people. The things that happen are things that happen to real people.

Read and Find *The Great Book Swap* is set in the present. The characters are realistic. The things that happen in the story are things that could happen in real life.

Your Turn

Imagine that you are moving. You can only keep some of your things. How would you reuse or recycle some of your things? Make the story realistic.